U.S. Mint

Miscellaneous Letters Received from 1897 to 1903

U.S. Mint

Miscellaneous Letters Received from 1897 to 1903

ISBN/EAN: 9783337817121

Printed in Europe, USA, Canada, Australia, Japan

Cover: Foto ©Suzi / pixelio.de

More available books at **www.hansebooks.com**

RG 104, 8KRA-104-84-042
Box 4, Volume VII

Miscellaneous Letters Received, 1897-1903.
Letters Received Relating   to the Construction
of the New Denver Mint, 1897-1906.

TREASURY DEPARTMENT,

OFFICE OF THE SUPERVISING ARCHITECT

Washington, March 21,1903.

Superintendent of Construction,
    New Mint,
       Denver, Colorado.

Sir:

    This Office is in receipt of a package marked raw linseed oil, forwarded by you and although no letter has been received relative thereto, it is presumed that it is a sample of the material delivered on the site of the building in your charge by Mr. James A. McGonigle, the contractor for the completion of the building. If such is the case, you are advised that while said sample does not contain adulteration, it has not been properly aged and settled and contains a large amount of foots and, therefore, you are directed to call the matter to the attention of the contractor and require him to remove from the premises any of such material which has been delivered and to supply material as represented by the approved sample, and upon such delivery you will forward a sample thereof to this Office for identification.

    There has also been received, under similar conditions, a can of red lead, which is satisfactory.

    In this connection you are directed, in the future, to forward with all samples a letter explanatory thereof.

        Respectfully,

              Supervising Architect

MTR

DENVER NEW MINT

F

2

3
/

March 23, 1905.

The Superintendent of Construction,

Mint Building (new),

Denver, Colorado.

17th instant

you are hereby authorized to incur an expenditure of thirty dollars ($30.00)

telephone service in Superintendent's office for a
period of three months from the 1st proximo, at
$10.00 per month, $ 30.00

, payment to be made from the
appropriation for "Mint Building,Denver,Colo."

DENVER. P.O.

B

TREASURY DEPARTMENT,

OFFICE OF THE SUPERVISING ARCHITECT,

Washington, March 24, 1903.

Mr. Lee Ullery,

     Superintendent of Construction,

          U. S. Mint (new),

               Denver, Colorado.

Sir:

     Referring to your report of the 19th instant, on the
matter of repairs and painting at the Post Office and Court
House, Denver, Colorado, and noting that only the original
is submitted, I have to advise you that it is desired that
all special reports with regard to repairs shall be in
duplicate.

          Respectfully,

                     Supervising Architect.

DENVER, NEW MINT

IN REPLYING TO THIS LETTER THE
INITIALS IN UPPER RIGHT-HAND
CORNER MUST BE REFERRED TO.

TREASURY DEPARTMENT,

OFFICE OF THE SUPERVISING ARCHITECT,

Washington, March 24,1903.

Superintendent of Construction,
    New Mint Building,
        Denver, Colorado.

Sir:

You are directed to obtain from the contractor for the
completion of the building under your charge a proposal for
using hard Alberene stone tiling 20" x 20" x 1 1/4", laid with
acid proof joints, in lieu of marble tiling called for under
his contract, for the assayer's, furnace and acid laboratories,
and forward the proposal to this Office as soon as possible,
together with a sample of the material upon which the proposal
is based and a statement as to the material to be used in join-
ing the same, with your definite recommendation.

Respectfully,

Supervising Architect.

D.A.C.

TREASURY DEPARTMENT,

OFFICE OF THE SUPERVISING ARCHITECT.

Washington, March 25, 1903.

Superintendent of Construction,

  U. S. Mint (new),

    Denver, Colorado.

Sir:

  In reply to your letter of the 21st instant, relative
to inspection of the work incident to the installation of the
mechanical equipment of the building for which you are Superintendent of Construction, you are advised that action has
already been taken by this Office looking to the detail of
an inspector to have charge of this work, and he will arrive
at the building early the coming month.

    Respectfully,

       Supervising Architect.

DENVER (new) MINT.

IN REPLYING TO THIS LETTER THE
INITIALS IN UPPER RIGHT-HAND
CORNER MUST BE REFERRED TO.
(FORWARDING)
(ENCL. 3006)

TREASURY DEPARTMENT,

OFFICE OF THE SUPERVISING ARCHITECT,

Washington,   March 25, 1903.

The Superintendent of Construction,

United States (new) Mint,

Denver, Colorado.

Sir:

There is enclosed herewith for information and
file a copy of office letter this day addressed to
Mr. James A. McGonigle, and, under separate cover, a
set of shop drawings Nos. 174 to 179 and 184 to 186,
both inclusive, therein mentioned in connection with
certain ornamental iron work to be supplied under
the contract for the interior finish of the building for which you are the Superintendent of Construction.

Respectfully,

Supervising Architect.

R.

(DENVER (his) MINT)

In REPLYING TO THIS LETTER THE
INITIALS IN UPPER RIGHT-HAND
CORNER MUST BE REFERRED TO.

FORWARDING)

EAC.

TREASURY DEPARTMENT,

OFFICE OF THE SUPERVISING ARCHITECT.

Washington, March 28, 1903,

Mr. James A. McGonigle,
    Care,Flour City Ornamental Iron Works,
        Minneapolis, Minnesota.

Sir:

The office is in receipt of your letter of the
22nd instant transmitting prints of shop drawings
for certain ornamental iron work to be supplied in
connection with the contract for the interior finish
of the New United States Mint Building,Denver,Colorado.

In reply you are advised that said drawings have
been given office Nos.174 to 179 and 184 to 186,both
inclusive,and one set of the prints has this day been
returned approved subject to the specification requirements and the corrections noted thereon in red.

In this connection attention is called to the
fact that these shop drawings must be prepared in
accordance with the full size details furnished by
this office,as it is evident from the many discrepancies which have occurred on the prints this day
returned that this course has not heretofore been
pursued.

Respectfully,

(SIGNED) J. K. TAYLOR,

Supervising Architect.

R.

DENVER (new) MINT.

IN REPLYING TO THIS LETTER THE
INITIALS IN UPPER RIGHT-HAND
CORNER MUST BE REFERRED TO.

ENCLOSURE 3007)

TREASURY DEPARTMENT,

OFFICE OF THE SUPERVISING ARCHITECT,

Washington,   March 27,1903.

The Superintendent of Construction,

United States (new) Mint,

Denver, Colorado.

Sir:

There is enclosed herewith a tracing showing a
slight correction in the section through the marble
cornice of the building for which you are the Superintendent of Construction,as indicated on the copy
of drawing #155 in your possession.

It was noted that there was a discrepancy between the section and plan of modillions,which has
been corrected on the above mentioned tracing,and,
after indicating said correction on the full size
detail in your possession,please deliver the tracing
to the contractor and instruct him to carry out the
work accordingly.

Respectfully,

Supervising Architect.

R.

DENVER, NEW MINT.

Superintendent of Construction,
  New Mint Building,
    Denver, Colorado.

Sir:

Referring to your letter of the 16th instant, forwarding
a proposal from Messrs. S. Faith & Company, the contractors
for the mechanical equipment of the building in your charge,
to put in the inspection pit beneath basement vault, a wrought
iron grille, vent duct, etc., you are hereby directed to
reject said proposal.

The proposal of James A. McGonigle, for doing this work
will form the subject of another communication.

Respectfully,

Supervising Architect.

MTR

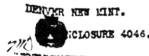

TREASURY DEPARTMENT,

OFFICE OF THE SUPERVISING ARCHITECT.

Washington, March 26, 1903.

Superintendent of Construction,
    New Mint Building,
        Denver, Colorado.

Sir:

I inclose herewith, for your information and the files
of your office, a copy of Department letter of even date, accepting the proposal of the contractor for the completion
of the building in your charge, in amount twenty-six dollars
and fifty cents ($26.50), for putting in place a vent flue
register, grille, etc., for pit below basement vault, as indicated on drawing #148, all as stated in detail in said
letter of acceptance, which explains itself.

You are hereby authorized to certify and issue vouchers
on account of the work, as required by the terms of the contract and the printed "Instructions to Superintendents", payment of which vouchers the Disbursing Agent has been authorized to make from the appropriation for Mint Building, Denver,
Colorado.

                    Respectfully,

                            Supervising Architect.

March 24,1903.

Mr.James A; McGonigle,
        Uniontown, Pennsylvania.

Sir;

In view of the statements and recommendation contained
in letter of March 19,1903, from the Superintendent of Construction of the new Mint building at Denver, Colorado, your
proposal, of the same date, addressed to him, in amount twenty-
six dollars and fifty cents ($26.50), is hereby accepted for
putting in place a vent flue register, grille,etc., for pit
below basement vault, as indicated on drawing #146, the amount
being deemed reasonable and a public exigency requiring the
immediate performance of the work, which is to be considered
as an addition to your contract, dated August 25,1902,for the
completion of the building.

It is understood and agreed that this undertaking is not
to affect the time for the completion of the entire work as
fixed in the original contract; that the same is without prejudice to me, and all rights of the United States hereunder;
and without prejudice, also, to the rights of the United States
against the sureties on the bond secured for the faithful
fulfillment of the contract.

Please promptly acknowledge the receipt of this letter.

                Respectfully,

                        Acting Secretary.

T.
JCP
MTF

TREASURY DEPARTMENT,

OFFICE OF THE SUPERVISING ARCHITECT

Washington,　March 25, 1903.

Superintendent of Construction,

　　U. S. Mint,

　　　　Denver, Colo.

Sir:-

　　Referring to your letter of the 17th instant, with regard to fitting up a room in the basement of the Post Office
and Court House building in your city, to provide additional
space for the files, etc., of the Money Order Division of the
Post Office, which is estimated to cost $800.00, I have to ad-
vise you that , in view of the expense involved, and the fact
as stated by you that the Post Office officials do not approve
of the scheme, no further action will be taken in the matter.

　　In view of your intimation that a mezzanine can be constructed for about $200.00 which may provide the necessary ad-
ditional space for files, I have to request that you will prepare a brief specification for the work, hand the same to the
Custodian of the building and request him to take proposals for
the performance of the work and to forward all received with
his recommendations as to acceptance. The bids should be check-
ed by you as to reasonableness before transmission to the Department.

　　　　　　　Respectfully,

　　　　　　　　　Supervising Architect.

TREASURY DEPARTMENT,

OFFICE OF THE SUPERVISING ARCHITECT.

Washington, March 28, 1903.

Superintendent of Construction,
     New Mint Building,
          Denver, Colorado.

Sir:

    I inclose herewith, for your information and the files
of your office, a copy of Department letter of even date,
accepting the proposal of Messrs. S.Faith & Company, the contractors for the mechanical equipment of the building in your
charge, to make certain substitution in circuit breakers and
instruments, without additional cost to the Government, all
as stated in detail in said letter of acceptance, which
explains itself.

                          Respectfully,

                                Supervising Architect.

MTR

March 28, 1903.

Messrs. P. Smith & Company,
  #2417 Pennsylvania Avenue,
    Philadelphia, Pa.

Gentlemen:

Your proposal, dated November 24, 1902, addressed
to the Supervising Architect of this Department, is hereby
accepted, to substitute circuit breakers manufactured by the
Cutter Electric Company in lieu of those made by the General
Incandescent Arc Light Company, on the main switchboard, and
Keystone registering instruments, such as voltmeters, ammeters,
and potential indicator, in lieu of the Weston instruments,
without additional cost to the Government, under your contract,
dated August 2, 1902, for the mechanical equipment of the
new Mint building at Denver, Colorado, a public exigency requiring the immediate performance of the work.

It is understood and agreed that this acceptance
is not to affect the time for the completion of the entire
work as fixed in the original contract; that the same is without prejudice to any and all rights of the United States
hereunder; and without prejudice, also, to the rights of the
United States against the sureties on the bond executed for
the faithful fulfillment of the contract.

Please promptly acknowledge the receipt of this letter.

Respectfully,

Acting Secretary.

T
JCP
MR

Denver, Colo., March 31st, 1903.

Mr.Lee Ullery, Superintendent,

U.S.Mint Building, City.

Dear Sir:-

Replying to your letter of March 25th, requesting us to submit to you an estimate of testing the eight (8) down spouts in the Mint Building, city, in order to ascertain the necessary repairs required to put all of them in perfect condition, would say that we have gone over this as carefully as possible under present conditions and we propose to make above tests as explained to us by you for the sum of One Hundred and Thirty-eight Dollars ($138.).

very respectfully,

S.Faith & Company,

Per Lewis.

BUFFALO FORGE COMPANY

ENGINEERS AND MANUFACTURERS
OF
BUFFALO HORIZONTAL AND VERTICAL AUTOMATIC ENGINES
FAN SYSTEM HEATING VENTILATING AND DRYING APPARATUS
STEEL PLATE STEAM, ELECTRIC AND PULLEY FANS
EXHAUST FANS AND VENTILATING WHEELS
CUPOLA AND FORGE BLOWERS
DOWN DRAFT SMOKE EXHAUST FORGES
HAND BLOWERS PORTABLE FORGES TIRE UPSETTERS
BLACKSMITH DRILLS, PUNCHES AND SHEARS

BUFFALO, NEW YORK Oct. 20, 1903.

United States Mint,

Denver, Colo.

Gentlemen:-   (Mechanical Draft)

Will you kindly inform us if the contract for Mechanical Draft
at your Mint recently arranged for was advertised in the U. S. Government
Advertiser, or in other papers? Was it also advertised in Denver papers?
If not, was the purchase made on open requisition?

Yours truly,

Dictated by Mr.   BUFFALO FORGE COMPANY.

'P

DENVER, NEW MINT

TREASURY DEPARTMENT,

OFFICE OF THE SUPERVISING ARCHITECT.

Washington, March 30, 1903.

The Superintendent of Construction,

  Mint Building,

    Denver, Colorado.

Sir:

  The Department has this day detailed Mr. Edward V. Roberts as Draftsman at the building under your charge at a compensation of $900.00 per year to commence on and include this day, and you are authorized to certify and issue vouchers for his services in accordance therewith, the Disbursing Agent having this day been advised and directed to make payment thereof. The traveling and subsistence expenses of Mr. Roberts from Washington, D.C., to Denver, Colo., will be paid, as a charge against the appropriation for "Mint Building, Denver, Colo.," upon vouchers to be forwarded to this Department.

      Respectfully,

        Acting Supervising Architect.

Printed Heading.

Denver, Colo., April 1st, 1903.

.L.Ullery, Supt.of Mint Building,

Denver, Colorado.

nr Sir:-

Your letter of March 31st asking for bid for steel furring
id expanded metal lathing for Attic story received. My bid for doing
ie work as specified will be $279.00.

Yours truly,

(Signed) James A.McGonigle.

Printed Heading.

Denver, Colo., April 2nd, 1903.

r.L.Ullery, Supt.of Mint Building,

Denver, Colorado.

Dear Sir :-

In reply to your letter asking me to submit bid for covering
floor of Coining room with magnesia magnaheetos and asbestos according
to plan submitted, the price for covering the entire coining room is
$ 1760.00,   Covering over boilers, $ 1194.00.

Respectfully,

(Signed) James A.McGonigle.

Philadelphia, Pa., December 15,1902.

Supervising Architect,

Washington, D.C.

:-

I desire to call your attention to the fact that the floor of the
Dining Room,Denver Mint Building, is as yet,un-insulated from the heat of
the boilers,which will be installed directly below the above mentioned room.

When I was at your drafting rooms,going over the Interior Finish work
before the contract for the same was put on the market,Mr.Adams,at my request,showed on the drawings a section of a compound floor construction according to the ideas that I thought should be followed. This construction
was not approved by your office and the section drawing was erased from the
prints, but I was given to understand that some future action would be tak-
en that would accomplish the desired result.

I am forwarding herewith a print,and correspondence relating thereto,
showing a method of floor construction that I wish to submit for approval.

The Philadelphia agent of the Keasbey & Mattison Co. has given me an
approximate price of not over $1400. for the whole area of coining room
floor (about 2000 sq.ft.) with the construction as proposed; this includes
all expenses of a man sent from Phila. to lay the work; that is,the asbestos,hard plaster and asphalted,asbestos paper laid in place ready to receive concrete and granolithic,as per print, for the above amount.

I earnestly recommend that a compound floor be laid rather than have
furred down ceiling installed in the boiler room,as was done at the Philadelphia Mint. In my opinion the furred ceiling,of asbestos air-cell fire

oard held in place by strap iron is a flimsy construction, has a short ife and does not accomplish the desired result.

The fact that the greater number of employees in the coining room are omen tends to emphasize the question of heat insulation for the room in uestion.

I would be pleased to receive a reply to this letter stating the robable action that will be taken.

Respectfully,

(Signed) F.E.Healy,

Engineer in Charge
Denver Mint Equipment.

Address: U.S.Mint,Phila,Pa.

Approved and forwarded.

Director of the Mint.

U. S. Mint, Denver, Colorado.

Coining Room Floor.

Present conditions: Concrete in place to top of eye-beams.

Recommend that magnahes'os blocks 6° x 36° x 1-1/2°,with 1/2° bevel, edges, be laid on concrete in place and wired,with copper wire,to the I-beams of floor construction; then cover magnashes'os blocks with a 1/4° well troweled coat of hard finish plaster; then lay one coat of asbestos paper roofing(this paper comes saturated with asphaltum),and allow the floor in that condition to season for two or three weeks before laying concrete and granolithic.

Approximate price for magnachestos blocks,plaster and paper in place not more than $1400.

The K.A.H.people say that for a floor figured for 300 lbs. per foot, as is the coining room floor steel work, that the compound construction will be as durable and as still under working loads as would concrete filling, and will be insulated in the best manner.

(Signed)   H e a l y.

Ambler, Pa., December 3,1902.

.P.R.Healy,

Engineer in Charge,Denver Mint Equipment,

U.S.Mint, Philadelphia, Pa.

Dear Sir:-

We beg to acknowledge the receipt of your valued favor of the 2nd instant, and in response to the same would say that we have carefully gone over your sketch and letter,and would suggest that instead of using Magnabestos,which you know is an ordinary and cheaper insulation,that you use our 85% Magnesia blocks which cost but a trifle more,and will give you probably double the service that you would receive from the magnabestos. When you order them,we would ask you to specify that these blocks shall be made of similar physical character to those manufactured for the lagging of locomotives,as these blocks are heavier and stronger than those ordinarily used for boiler covering. When you order them,if you will specify that they shall have 1/2" bevel,then the blocks can be so tightly driven together that you will not have any joints to fill up between them,and the insulation will be as complete and perfect in character as it is possible to make it,on account of the joints being broken by the beveled edges of the blocks. We think it would be an advantage if you would cover the blocks after they are wired down to the floor beams,with a roll of Asbestos paper roofing,which you know is saturated with asphaltum,and which would prevent the water,from the 1/4" covering of hard plaster which you propose to put upon the blocks, from being absorbed by the Magnesia. Of course,it will not hurt the Magnesia to absorb this water,as it will eventually dry out anyway,and the Magnesia will be just as good as it was before the water and plaster were applied, and any moisture which comes through from the concrete flooring above, by accident, will also eventually dry out, and the Magnesia insulation will not be in any way affected by the fact of its having been wet.

Trusting we will have your orders for whatever you may need in this connection, we remain

Respectfully yours,

Keasby & Mattison Co.,

W. Richard V. Mattison, M.D.,

President & General Manager.

Philadelphia, December 10,1902.

Mr.P.R.Henly,

　　Engineer in Charge Denver Mint Equipment,

　　　　c/o Philadelphia Mint.

Dear Sir:-

　　We are in receipt of a blue print from you showing the construction
of a flooring which you propose placing in the New Mint at Denver, Colo.,
and after giving the same our careful consideration,we beg to advise that
we think the mode of construction as set forth therein,will be most efficient as to durability and non-conductivity.　We note that you propose
to use the K.& M.(85%) Magnesia blocks, or 35% Magnabestos blocks,placing
over same as Asbestos Sheathing Paper, the joints between the blocks to be
filled in with a dry grout of same composition as the blocks.　This construction would not be very expensive,and as we have stated above,would
be very durable and efficient,and we strongly endorse its adoption.

　　　　　　　　Yours very truly,

　　　　　　　　　Magnesia Covering Company,

　　　　　　　　　　Barclay Johnson

　　　　　　　　　　Secretary & Gen.Mgr.

TREASURY DEPARTMENT,

OFFICE OF THE SUPERVISING ARCHITECT.

Washington, **March** 31, 1903.

The Superintendent of Construction,

　　Mint Building,

　　　　Denver, Colorado.

Sir:

　　Office letter of the 30th instant, informing you of the detail of Mr. Edward W. Roberts, as Draftsman at the building under your charge is hereby amended and modified by conveying the information that the oath of office is taken this day, on which date his compensation will commence.

　　　　　　　　　Respectfully,

　　　　　　　　　　　　Acting Supervising Architect.

PUEBLO.

Mr. Lee Ullery,

    Superintendent of Construction, &c.,

        New Mint Building,

           Denver, Colorado.

Sir:

    An agreement is in force with The Piper Brothers Company, for certain repairs, &c., at the Post-Office building, at Pueblo, Colorado, and you are requested to make two visits to the building named, in order to examine and report upon the work, full information in regard to which will be found on the Custodian's files; your first visit to be so timed as to secure the best results, and the second visit at such date as will enable you to make final examination and report upon the work.

    The Custodian has been advised of your detail and he has been requested to communicate with you in order that you may determine the probable date of your first visit.

    Upon completion of your duties at each visit, return to Denver, Colorado, and submit reports of the results thereof, checking any vouchers issued by the Custodian in payment for the work.

    Your actual traveling and subsistence expenses while in the performance of these duties will be paid from appropria-

DENVER, NEW MINT.

Inclosure 2804.

Superintendent of Construction,
   New Mint Building,
      Denver, Colorado.

Sir:

I inclose herewith, for your information and the files of
your office, a copy of Department letter of even date, formally
accepting the proposal of S. Faith & Company, in amount one hundred and thirty-eight dollars ($138.00), for testing eight
down spouts on the building in your charge, all as stated in
the said letter of acceptance, this to be considered as independent
of their contract for the mechanical equipment of the building.

You are hereby authorized to certify and issue vouchers on
account of the work, upon Form 12B, after its completion by the
contractors, and acceptance by the Government, payment of which
vouchers the Disbursing Agent has been authorized to make from
the appropriation for Mint Building, Denver, Colorado.

                              Respectfully,

                                          Supervising Architect.

JSS

... .Peirce & Co.,
... Int Willing,
..., California.

...:

In view of the statement in recommendation contained
... ... of the first letter, from the superintendent of construction of the new ... Pacific, Denver, Chicago, ... in accordance with the approval of this agreement, ...,
... the same data, ... to the, ... one ...
... . Oakland ($150.00), is hereby ... ... to
... ... with ... of the said ..., in order to locate
... ... legal ..., a public ... ... the ...
... ... of the form, which is to be ... to the entire
satisfaction of the department, and to be considered as in-
... ... your contract for the ... ... of the
...

This letter is a continuation of the ... ...
... the 4th letter, as follows:

   "... ... ...,
    ... ...,
    ... ..."

... on ... of the ... ...
... of the ... ... to the ..., ... to ap-
... ...

... ...

Office of Custodian

U. S. COURT HOUSE AND POST OFFICE,

Pueblo, Colo., April 10, 1903.

Lee Ullery,

Sup't of Construction U.S. Mint Building,

Denver, Colorado.

Dear Sir:

Yours of 9th inst. at hand, and your kindness in furnishing the drawing is fully appreciated. It is exactly what I needed, as it will make the condition clear to the Department and also enable me to get intelligent estimates on the cost of the improvement if authorized. Mr. Morgan, who looked at the drawing this morning, says it shows how to remedy the trouble directly and effectually. His only suggestion by way of amendment was that 6-lb. lead would be more satisfactory than 3-lb. for the purpose designated.

Respectfully,

(signature)

Custodian.

Mr. L. Miller Supt of Mint Building
Chicago

Dear Sir
I am in
letter recd from ... Marble & Proctor
... in regard to details of Marble
work claiming that the details are not
according to original drawings Not
having here details here I cannot
... — Will you please look the
matter over and let me know —
... letter

Proctor,Vt., April 2nd,1903.

'Ir.James A.McGonigle,

    Leavenworth,Kansas.   Denver Mint.

Dear Sir:-

    There is a big discrepancy between the original drawings on which we estimated for you and on the full sized details that you have furnished us for the marble cornice for this job. Under another cover we are sending you a tracing explaining fully what we mean. The original drawings in several instances indicate that the under sides of the modillions,etc.,are simply to have sunk disks,while the full sizes that you furnish us call for work of a very different character and of great deal more expense to us. We ask that you have the full size detail changed to agree with the original drawings. Kindly give this your early attention.

          Yours truly,

            Vermont Marble Company. D.H.B.

22

April 10th, 1903.

Mr. Lee Ullery,

    Superintendent of Construction,

        New Mint Building, Denver, Colorado.

Sir:-

    In arranging for cutting the stonework for the wall on the south line of lot at the Mint building, in this city, I find that its west end is nearly 5'10" lower than the east end (due to the fall in grade of the alley), and that a note on drawing No.122 requires a batter of 1" in 1'6" height of said wall.

    Owing to the difference in levels of the two ends, it does not seem possible to construct the wall with a batter throughout its entire height and yet have the stonework finish at a uniform thickness to receive the coping.

    I suggest that the wall be constructed with a base of the thickness indicated on drawing No.122 with a batter from the said base to the line of joint directly beneath the coping at the west end of the wall, at which height the wall would be 2'0 1/2" in thickness throughout its entire length, the portion of the wall above that joint line to be 2'0 1/2" thick and have both faces plumb. The coping to be of the same dimensions as shown and noted on the drawings.

    If this meets the approval of the Department, I will perform the work according to the said arrangement without additional expense to the Government.

                Respectfully,

                  James A. McDonigle,

                      Contractor.

TREASURY DEPARTMENT
OFFICE OF THE SUPERVISING ARCHITECT

Washington, April 9, 1903.

Enclosure No. 4866.

Superintendent of Construction,
     U.S. Mint Building (new),
          Denver, Colorado.

Sir:

I enclose herewith, for your information and the files of your office, copy of a letter this day addressed to Mr. James A. McGonigle, contractor for the construction of the building in your charge, relative to the approval of certain samples of enameled brick proposed to be used in connection with such contract. There is also forwarded you, under separate cover, sample of the enameled brick therein referred to, for the files of your office and for your guidance in accepting the work.

Respectfully,

Supervising Architect.

April 8, 190_.

Mr. James A. McConigle,
      Denver, Colorado.

Sir:

I have to acknowledge the receipt of your letter, without date, received at ... under separate cover ...

[illegible]

TREASURY DEPARTMENT,
OFFICE OF THE SUPERVISING ARCHITECT.

Washington, April 9, 1903.

Superintendent of Construction,
    New Mint,
        Denver, Colorado.

Sir:

I inclose herewith, for your information and the files
of your office, a copy of a letter this day addressed to the
contractor for the completion of the building in your charge,
which letter explains itself, and the sample of marble, mentioned therein as being approved for use in the work, where
required, is forwarded you, under separate cover, being for
the files of your office and your guidance in accepting the
work.

                Respectfully,

                            Supervising Architect.

DENVER MINT.

April 9, 1901.

Mr. James A. McDaniels,
    New Mint Building,
        Denver, Colorado.

Sir:

This Office is in receipt of a letter of the 6th instant
under heading of the Vermont Marble Company, submitting an
additional sample of marble with more distinct veining for
wall work in connection with your contract for the completion
of the new Mint building at Denver, Colorado, and you are advised that this sample is approved, in addition to the one
approved on the 6 ultimo, and the sample has been forwarded
to the Superintendent of Construction for the files of his
office and his guidance in executing the work.

Respectfully,

Supervising Architect.

DENVER NEW MINT.

ENCLOSURE 3147.   **TREASURY DEPARTMENT,**

OFFICE OF THE SUPERVISING ARCHITECT.

Washington, April 9, 1903.

Superintendent of Construction,
     New Mint,
          Denver, Colorado.

Sir:

I inclose herewith, for your information and the files

of your office, a copy of a letter this day addressed to the

contractor for the completion of the building in your charge,

relative to granite, which letter explains itself.

Respectfully,

Supervising Architect.

April 5, ----.

----- ---, ---------,
     ---- -----------,
          ------, Colorado.

Sir:

I have to acknowledge the receipt of your letter of the 4th instant, in which you request the approval under your contract for the completion of the new Mint building at Denver, Colorado, a sample of ----- ----- granite which has been accepted ---- ---- previous contract for other work in this building, and I am of opinion that it has been decided, as represented by the sample submitted by J. ------, are approved under the contract, is approved of the ------ granite ---- ---- --------- is required under your contract, and the ----------- ---- of Construction ---- ---- ---- advised.

                              ------ ---ll.,

                                        Supervising Architect.

Printed Heading.

Denver, Colo., April 13th, 1903.

Superintendent of Construction,

U.S.Mint Building, City.

Dear Sir:-

In reply to your letter of the 11th instant.

We propose to repair the down pipes now in place and the copper gutter lining at the U.S.Mint Building, using additional pipe where necessary to substitute for that broken, raise the pipe where necessary and do all necessary refilling and calking of the joints, including the connection to the roof gutter where necessary and resolder all defective joints in the present copper gutter lining, so as to make the gutters and down pipes water-tight and stand a test made by us by filling the pipes and gutter with water and allowed to stand three hours, all for the sum of TWO HUNDRED AND TWENTY-FOUR DOLLARS ($224.00).

Respectfully,

S.Faith & Company,

Per Lewis.

TREASURY DEPARTMENT,

OFFICE OF THE SUPERVISING ARCHITECT.

Washington, April 11, 1903.

The Superintendent of Construction,

United States Mint (New),

Denver, Colorado.

Sir:

You are advised that Mr. N. S. Thompson, Inspector of
Heating, Hoisting and Ventilating Apparatus, of this Office,
has been detailed to the building for which you are Superintendent of Construction, to take charge of the supervision
and inspection of the work being installed by S. Faith & Co.,
of Philadelphia, Pennsylvania, in connection with their contract for the mechanical equipment of said building, and will
arrive there on or about the 15th instant.

The inspector is to submit to this Office, through you,
weekly reports on the character of workmanship and material
supplied, and progress made, in connection with above contract;
and you are requested to afford him such facilities in the way
of desk room, stationery, access to your files, etc., as may
be necessary for the proper discharge of his duties.

Respectfully,

DENVER MINT (NEW).

(ENCLOSURE #2743)
FORWARDING.

TREASURY DEPARTMENT.

OFFICE OF THE SUPERVISING ARCHITECT.

EAC.

Washington, April 13, 1903.

The Superintendent of Construction,

    United States Mint Building (New),

        Denver, Colorado.

Sir:

    There is enclosed herewith for information and file
a copy of Office letter this day addressed to Mr. James
A. McGonigle, and, under separate cover, two prints of drawing No.187, therein mentioned, showing certain granite work
to be supplied in connection with the interior finish for
the building of which you are the Superintendent of Construction.

        Respectfully,

                  Supervising Architect.

B.

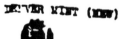

DENVER MINT (NEW)

(FORWARDING)

TREASURY DEPARTMENT,

OFFICE OF THE SUPERVISING ARCHITECT

Washington, April 13, 1903.

EAC.

Mr. James A. McConigle,

United States Mint Building,

Denver, Colorado.

Sir:

The receipt of your letter of the 8th instant, transmitting, in quadruplicate, shop drawing showing certain granite work to be supplied under your contract for the interior finish of the new U.S. Mint Building at Denver, Colorado, is hereby acknowledged, and in reply you are advised that said drawing has been given Office number 187 and one print of same has this day been returned to you, under separate cover, approved subject to the corrections noted thereon in red.

The foregoing approval is, however, general in character, referring only to the position and location of the joints, all responsibility for fitting and measurements being assumed by you.

Respectfully,

(Signed) J. K. TAYLOR,

Supervising Architect.

B.

29

DENVER,NEW MINT.

Inclosure 2760.

TREASURY DEPARTMENT,

OFFICE OF THE SUPERVISING ARCHITECT.

Washington, April 14,1903.

Superintendent of Construction,
New Mint Building,
Denver,Colorado.

Sir:

I inclose herewith, for your information and the files of
your office, a copy of Department letter of even date, accepting
the proposal of Mr. James A.McGonigle, the contractor for the
completion of the building in your charge, in amount two hundred
and seventy-nine dollars ($279.00), for placing steel furring
and expanded metal lathing to receive the plastering in rooms
in attic, in lieu of plastering directly on soffits of book
tile as specified.

You are hereby authorized to certify and issue vouchers on
account of this addition, as required by the terms of the contract and the printed "Instructions to Superintendents", payment of which vouchers the Disbursing Agent has been authorized
to make from the appropriation for Mint Building,Denver,Colorado.

Respectfully,

JSS

Supervising Architect.

DENVER, NOT SENT.

April 14, 1903

Mr. ....McCormick,
..... .-. ....,
Denver, Colorado.

Sir:

In view of the statement and recommendation contained in letter of ...., from the Superintendent of Construction of .... mayor, Boettcher, and in accordance with the approval of this department, ..., dated the 1st instant, a copy ...., by which two hundred and ninety-.......... dollars ($ .....), is hereby accepted to .... total letting if .... of the said ...., to .... directly on the .... 1903, in accordance with the terms of the specifications .... of the ...., and ...., ... delivery requiring the ....of the ......, and is to be .... to .... contract, dated ....,1903 for the completion of the ....

It is .... that .... to .... the .... for the completion of .... by the .... of your contract; but the same is .... all right of ...., also, to any and all right of .... the sureties on the bond executed for the faithful fulfillment of the contract.

Please acknowledge the receipt of this letter, a copy of which will be forwarded to the Superintendent of the mills.

Respectfully,

Assistant Secretary.

DENVER, NEW MINT,

Inclosure 2761.

TREASURY DEPARTMENT,
OFFICE OF THE SUPERVISING ARCHITECT.

Washington, April 14, 1902.

Superintendent of Construction,
   New Mint Building,
     Denver, Colorado.

Sir:

I inclose herewith, for your information and the files of
your office, a copy of Department letter, of even date, accepting
the proposal of James A. McGonigle, the contractor for the completion of the building in your charge, to lay magnabestos
blocks in that portion of the coining room floor that is over
boiler room, for the additional sum of one thousand one hundred
and ninety-four dollars ($1,194.CC), as stated.

You are hereby authorized to certify and issue vouchers on
account of this addition, as required by the terms of the contract and the printed "Instructions to Superintendents", payment
of which vouchers the Disbursing Agent has been authorized to
make from the appropriation for Mint Building, Denver, Colorado.

              Respectfully,

                          Supervising Architect.

JEE

View of the statement and recommendation contained in the enclosed, from the Department of construction ... Denver, Colorado, and in accordance with ... Department, your report, of the same date,

...

DENVER MINT (NEW).   51

Superintendent of Construction,
   United States Mint Building (New),
      Denver, Colorado.
Sir:

    I have to acknowledge the receipt of your letter of the
7th instant, relative to vent flues from basement toilet room
near column number four, and you are directed to procure bids
from Mr. McGonigle to construct a double partition in basement
between columns four and five, shown on drawing No.100 for the
introduction of certain heating and vent flues referred to in
your letter, and you are advised that register openings in
locker room and gas generating plant in basement are to be
placed twelve inches above floor and the registers are to be
16" x 18". Upon receipt of the above mentioned proposal,
with your definite recommendation, prompt action will be taken
by this Office.

                Respectfully,

                        Supervising Architect.

FOP

DENVER, NEW MINT.

MOD

FORWARDING.
ENCLOSURE 2605.

TREASURY DEPARTMENT

OFFICE OF THE SUPERVISING ARCHITECT

Washington, April 17, 1903.

The Superintendent of Construction,

U. S. Mint (new),

Denver, Col.

Sir:

For your information find herewith copy of office letter of
this date, addressed to Messrs. S. Faith and Company, contractors
for mechanical equipment of the building for which you are the Superintendent of Construction, advising them of approval of sample
of White Vermont marble to be used incident to plumbing work.

The approved sample will be forwarded to you to-day, by express, charges prepaid.

Respectfully,

Supervising Architect.

April 27, 1908.

Messrs. C. White and Company,

                407 Pennsylvania Ave.,

    P   Philadelphia, Pa.

    Sir:

        Receipt is acknowledged of your letter of April 4th 1908,
    transmitting sample of White Vermont Marble, for consideration in
    connection with plumbing work under your contract for mechanical
    equipment of the U.S. Mint (new), Denver, Col., and you are ad-
    vised that said sample has been forwarded to
    the Custodian at Denver.

                    Respectfully,

                (Signed)   J. K. TAYLOR,

                        Supervising Architect.

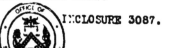

INCLOSURE 3087.   **TREASURY DEPARTMENT**

WASHINGTON, April 1?, 19?3.

Superintendent of Construction,
    New Mint,
        Denver, Colorado.

Sir:

    I inclose herewith, for your information and the files
of your office, a copy of Department letter of even date, accepting the proposal of Mr. James A. McGonigle, the contractor
for the completion of the building in your charge, to make
certain modification in the manner of using batter in the rear
retaining wall of the building, without extra expense to the
Government, all as stated in detail in said letter of acceptance, which explains itself.

               Respectfully,

                              Supervising Architect.

JOB.

LTR

April 17, 190..

Mr. James A. McGonigle,
New Mint Building,
Denver, Colorado.

Sir:

In view of the statements and recommendation contained in letter of April 11, 190.., from the Superintendent of construction of the New Mint Building at Denver, Colorado, your proposal, dated April 10, 190.., addressed to him, is hereby accepted, to modify the rear retaining wall so as to use batter as indicated on sketch forwarded by you in lieu of as shown on drawing #122, without additional cost to the Government, under your contract, dated August 25, 1902, for the completion of the building, a public exigency requiring this change in the work.

It is understood and agreed that this acceptance is not to affect the time for the completion of the entire work as fixed in the original contract; that the same is without prejudice to any and all rights of the United States thereunder; and without prejudice, also, to the rights of the United States against the sureties on the bond executed for the faithful fulfillment of the contract.

Please promptly acknowledge the receipt of this letter, a copy of which will be forwarded to the Superintendent of Construction, for his information.

Respectfully,

Assistant Secretary.

T
JCP

MTR

DENVER, NEW MINT
S3P

TREASURY DEPARTMENT,

OFFICE OF THE SUPERVISING ARCHITECT.

Washington, April 18, 1903.

F.B.I.

Superintendent of Construction,

    U. S. Mint (New),

        Denver, Colorado.

Sir:

    In reply to your letter of the 14th instant, relative
to placing the name of Inspector Thompson, detailed to your
building to take charge of the supervision and inspection of
work incident to the mechanical equipment, upon the pay roll
of contingent force of the building, you are advised that the
name of said inspector is not to go upon the roll referred to.

        Respectfully,

                    Supervising Architect.

DENVER NEW MINT.

(ENCLOSURE 3025)

The Superintendent of Construction,

United States (new) Mint,

Denver, Colorado.

Sir:

There is enclosed herewith for information and
file a copy of certain correspondence which has pass-
ed between this office and Mr. J. A. McGonigle, together with a tracing of drawing #155-B therein mentioned in connection with the marble cornice in the
corridor of the building for which you are the superintendent of construction, and you will please be
governed accordingly.

Respectfully,

Supervising Architect.

R.

April 21st, 1903.

To the Supervising Architect,

Treasury Department, Washington, D.C.

Sir:-

Referring to your letter dated November 14th, 1902, in which you state that the cast iron soil pipe we now have on the premises of the U.S.Mint Building, Denver, may be used if the coating is burned off we desire to say that we find it impossible to burn off the coating and make the pipe in any way resemble the uncoated pipe, nor does it permit of a more perfect inspection than is the case prior to the burning process.

In ordering this pipe we failed to order the uncoated expressly and as the coated pipe is used exclusively in the west we were furnished pipe as used in this section.

Our experience has been that extra heavy cast iron pipe contains practically no blow holes or other imperfections and we believe that the coating does not prohibit a proper inspection.

The defects, if any exist, in the pipe would be detected by the hydrostatic pressure test even if surface inspection failed to detect them.

In view of the fact that all of this pipe is underground we believe that the coating will act as a preservative and be an advant-

We acknowledge our mistake in ordering the pipe and we hereby propose to deduct the sum of ONE HUNDRED DOLLARS ($100.00) from our contract price if permitted to use the coated cast iron pipe in lieu of the uncoated pipe required by the terms of the agreement.

We understand that this change in the contract, if permitted, will not affect the time of completion.

Respectfully,

(Signed) S.Faith & Co.,
Lewis.

P.S.Please wire decision at our expense.

S.Faith & Co.,
L.

U. S. COURT HOUSE AND POST OFFICE,

Pueblo, Colo., April 21, 1903.

Mr. Les Ullery,

Sup't of Construction U.S. Mint Building,

Denver, Colorado.

Sir:--

With reference to the two window areas on the west side of this building, the specifications for the work now being done by The Piper Bros. Co. have this to say:

"Before laying the floors in the areas, as hereinafter specified, the bell traps must be carefully jointed to the drains; using brass sleeves if necessary, and the joints to be lead calked water tight. The traps in the two window areas on the west side of the building are to be connected as above specified, if the Custodian so require; the area floors to be properly repaired thereafter."

As the floors of these window areas need no repairs, and the bell traps are said not to leak, I was of opinion that the traps need not be taken up; but Mr. Morton, the janitor, has an impression that you instructed him to see that those traps were taken up and reset with solder jointing. Kindly inform me on this point.

Respectfully,

[signature]

Custodian.

DENVER NEW MINT.

INCLOSURE 3090.

TREASURY DEPARTMENT

WASHINGTON April 20, 1903.

Superintendent of Construction,
   New Mint,
      Denver, Colorado.

Sir:

    I inclose herewith, for your information and the files
of your office, a copy of a letter this day addressed to the
contractor for the completion of the building in your charge,
relative to a sample of terrazzo, which letter explains itself.

        Respectfully,

               Supervising Architect.

MTR

Mr. James _____ ,
_____ Building,
Denver, Colorado.

I beg to acknowledge the receipt of your letter of the
_____ instant, submitting sample to _____ in connection
with _____ contract for the completion of the _____ building at Denver, Colorado, and am advised that _____,
_____ by the sample, is rejected, inasmuch as specification requires for _____ sample _____ a colored sample.

In this connection your attention is called to letter
addressed to you on the 21st ultimo relative to the specification requirements in regard to the submission of samples,
together with the fact that up to the present time no attention appears to have been paid to said letter.

Respectfully,

Supervising Architect.

Printed Heading.

Denver, Colo., April 23rd, 1903

To the

Supervising Architect,

Treasury Department, Washington, D.C.

Sir:-

Referring to paragraphs Nos.11,23 and 24 of the specification governing our contract for the installation of the Mechanical Equipment (except engines and generators) in this building, we desire to herewith make claims for extension of the date for the completion of the work; which date for completion was March 25th,1903.

The condition of the building did not permit our completing our work within the stipulated time.

The placing of the interior finish of the building is causing us delay and said work is advancing so slowly that we are not warranted securing a more rapid advancement of the Mechanical Equipment.

The delays in the completion of our contract are due to causes beyond our control and we request that in accordance with paragraph No.11 of the specification that consideration be given to this fact at the time of final settlement.

Respectfully,

(Signed) S.Pnith & Co.,
for Lewis.

TREASURY DEPARTMENT

OFFICE OF THE SUPERVISING ARCHITECT

P.B.X.

Washington, April 21, 1903.

The Superintendent of Construction,

  U. S. Mint (New),

    Denver, Col.

Sir:

  Replying to your letter of the 14th instant, referring to drawing # 124 forming part of contract for construction of the building for which you are the Superintendent, you are advised that arrangement of openings for flues near column #0, as indicated on said drawing, is incorrect, and that flues must be installed as shown on drawings numbered 101, 102, and 109, floor framing to be arranged accordingly.

    Respectfully,

        Supervising Architect.

DENVER NEW MINT.

Inclosure 2779.

TREASURY DEPARTMENT,

OFFICE OF THE SUPERVISING ARCHITEC

Washington, April 22,1903.

Superintendent of Construction,
    New Mint Building,
        Denver,Colorado.

Sir:

I inclose herewith, for your information and the files of
your office, a copy of Department letter of even date, accepting
the proposal of S.Faith & Company, in amount two hundred and
twenty-four dollars ($224.00), for putting in good condition
the roof gutter and down pipes of the building in your charge,
this to be considered as independent of their contract for the
mechanical equipment of the building.

You are hereby authorized to certify and issue vouchers
on account of the work, upon Form 128, after its completion by
the contractors and acceptance by the Government,payment of
which vouchers the Disbursing Agent has been authorized to make
from the appropriation for Mint Building,Denver,Colorado.

                                    Respectfully,

                                    Supervising Architect.

JSS

April 23, 1900,

Hon. ... .,
.... Building,
......ver, Colorado.

Gentlemen,

In view of the .... and recommendation enclosed
in letter of the 14th instant, from the Superintendent of Construction of the new Mint Building, Denver, Colorado, and in accordance with the approval of this Department, some ....,
dated the ...th instant, addressed to me, in amount two ....
and twenty-four dollars ($24.00), is hereby accepted as ... in
a ....in the agreement as the ...... fitter of the builder,
in .... with the ... of ...... ,19.. and to the entire
satisfaction of the Superintendent, a public exigency requiring
the .... performance of the work, which is to be considered
independent of your contract for the mechanical equipment of
the building.

Payment on account of the work will be made, after
its completion by you and acceptance by the government, from the
appropriation for Mint Building, Denver, Colorado.

Respectfully,

Acting Secretary.

TREASURY DEPARTMENT,

OFFICE OF THE SUPERVISING ARCHITECT.

Washington,   April 21, 1903.

F.B.V.

The Superintendent of Construction,

United States Mint Building,

Denver, Colorado.

Sir:

There is enclosed herewith for information and file
a copy of Office letter this day addressed to Mr. James
A. McGonigle, and, under separate cover, two sets of shop
drawings Nos. 188 to 196, inclusive, therein mentioned, for
certain ornamental iron work to be supplied in connection
with the building for which you are the Superintendent of
Construction.

Respectfully,

Supervising Architect.

B.

DIVISION IV (NEW)

(FORWARDING)

TREASURY DEPARTMENT

OFFICE OF SUPERVISING ARCHITECT.

Washington, April 21, 1903.

Mr. James A. McGonigle,

Leavenworth, Kansas.

Sir:

The Office is in receipt of your letter of the 17th instant, transmitting, in quadruplicate, shop drawings for the iron grilles for exterior doors and windows and for the iron lamps and balconies to be supplied in connection with your contract for the new United States Mint Building at Denver, Colorado, and in reply you are advised that said drawings have been given Office numbers 188 to 196, inclusive, and one set of the prints has this day been returned to you, under separate cover, approved subject to the specification requirements regarding fitting, measurements, etc., and the corrections noted thereon in red.

Respectfully,

(Signed) J. K. TAYLOR,

Supervising Architect.

B.

DENVER MINT (NEW)

TREASURY DEPARTMENT,

OFFICE OF THE SUPERVISING ARCHITECT.

Washington,   April 21,1903.

The Superintendent of Construction,

United States Mint Building,

Denver,Colorado.

Sir:

In reply to your communication of April 16th in
reference to the approval of shop drawing No.187 for the
building of which you are the Superintendent of Construction,on which certain coping was indicated as 2' 3" in
width,you are informed that an error was made in check-
ing this drawing,2' 0-1/2" being the correct width of
the coping on walls along South Thirteenth Street,Evans
Street and Colfax Avenue,and 2' 3" for the coping on rear
retaining wall.

Respectfully,

Supervising Architect.

DENVER NEW MINT.

TREASURY DEPARTMENT

WASHINGTON April 22, 1903.

Superintendent of Construction,
New Mint,
Denver, Colorado.

Sir:

I have to acknowledge the receipt of your letter of the 16th instant, in which you state that the contractor for the completion of the building in your charge, Mr.McGonigle, is unable to find the name of parties who can furnish Alberne stone and you are advised that it is understood that the Alberne Stone Company of New York City can furnish the stone.

Respectfully,

Supervising Architect.

DENVER NEW MINT.

(ENCLOSURE 3035)

TREASURY DEPARTMENT,

OFFICE OF THE SUPERVISING ARCHITECT.

Washington,   April 24, 1903.

The Superintendent of Construction,

f   United States (new) Mint,

Denver, Colorado.

Sir:

In reply to your letter of the 21st instant, there is enclosed herewith a copy of the correspondence, referred to in office letter of the 18th instant in relation to drawing #155-B for the marble cornice in the corridor of the building for which you are the superintendent of construction, which you state has been lost in transmission.

Respectfully,

(Supervising Architect.

R.

DENVER NEW MINT.

(ENCLOSURE 3024)

Mr. J. A. McGonigle,

    Leavenworth,Kansas.

Sir:

    In reply to your communication of April 14th, transmitting a letter to you from the Vermont Marble Company of April 2nd,in reference to a discrepancy between the contract drawings and the full size details for the marble cornice in the corridor of the new United States Mint Building,Denver,Colorado,you are informed that there is herewith enclosed a tracing of full size detail drawing #155-B,showing the detail of this modillion in accordance with the contract drawings,and you are directed to carry out the work in accordance therewith.

              Respectfully,

                (Signed) J. K. Taylor,

                  Supervising Architect.

R.

PROCTOR,VT., April 2, 1903.

Mr. James A. McGonigle,

      Leavenworth,Kans.   Denver Mint.

Dear Sir:

      There is a big discrepancy between the original drawings on which we estimated for you and on the full size details that you have furnished us for the marble cornice for this job. Under another cover we are sending you a tracing explaining fully what we mean. The original drawings in several instances indicate that the under sides of the modillions,etc. are simply to have sunk disks, while the full size details that you furnish us call for work of a very different character and of a great deal more expense to us. We ask that you have the full size detail changed to agree with the original drawings. Kindly give this your early attention.

                        Yours truly,

                            Vermont Marble Co.

Leavenworth,Kansas, April 14,1903.

Mr. J. Knox Taylor,

Supervising Architect,

Washington.

Dear Sir:

I enclose a letter from the Vermont Marble Company of Proctor claiming there is a discrepancy between the original drawings and the full size details afterwards furnished.

Will you please examine into it and let me know.

Yours truly,

(Signed) James A. McGonigle.

TREASURY DEPARTMENT

WASHINGTON ,April 22,1903.

Superintendent of Construction,
New Mint,
Denver, Colorado.

Sir:

I have to acknowledge the receipt of your letter of the 26th ultimo and, under separate cover, of the sample of linseed oil, taken from material delivered on the site of the building in your charge, and you are advised that the same has been tested and found to be satisfactory.

Respectfully,

Supervising Architect.

DENVER, NEW MINT.

(ENCLOSURE #3177)

P.B.W.

The Superintendent of Construction,

United States Mint Building,

Denver, Colorado.

Sir:

There is enclosed herewith for information and file
a copy of Office letter of this date addressed to Mr.
James A. McGonigle, relative to certain work to be supplied
under his contract for the interior finish of the building
for which you are the Superintendent of Construction, which
will explain itself.

Respectfully,

Supervising Architect.

B.

Mr. J. A. McGonigle,
   Uniontown,
      Fayette County,
         Pennsylvania.

Sir:

In accordance with your verbal request of April 27th, the following information in explanation of two inquiries forwarded to you by your sub-contractor for mill work in the United States new Mint Building, Denver, Colorado, is herewith transmitted.

1. Sash generally are to be 1-3/4" thick; but the sash in window "C", first story, should be 2" thick, as figured on contract drawing #114.

2. Full size detail drawing #167 may be followed as regards detail of moulding in getting out sashes.

3. The T irons called for on page #34 of the specifications are intended to be placed in the meeting rails of the sashes, and it was not intended that these should be placed in the bottom rails.

4. The strip on frame for pivoted inside sash should be secured to the frame as specified.

5. A 7/8" base may be used in all cases where not otherwise shown on contract drawings.

6 & 7. In many cases the wood finish is shown as a whole - not detailed in pieces - the question of jointing being left to the judgment of the contractor.

9. Door moulding may be narrowed 1/4"; members being adjusted to this change; this moulding to be mailed to the saline.

11. You have been furnished with full size details Nos. 140 to 173, inclusive, and Nos. 153-A and 153-B for marble work, and it is believed that these details cover all the various items referred to by your sub-contractors.

The following information is,however,included for the
information of your sub-contractors:

BASEMENT:

    Doors T,U and U' may be made similar to window F',
drawing #151.

    Arched openings near staircase are in plaster;
no full size details are required.

    Iron gates A and B are shown on drawing #17.

    Doors O and O' are similar to M',drawing #150.

    Folding gates are not detailed; shop drawings
for same being required.

    Doors N and P are similar to M',drawing #150.

    Windows P-2 and P-3 are similar to P,drawing
No.151; see also scale drawing #117.

FIRST FLOOR:

    Door B is similar to A-1,drawing #150.

    Doors D,D-1 and D-2,similar to C,drawing 4.

    Folding door to lift #3,similar to A',sheet #.

    Closet door on balcony similar to C,drawing #.

    Windows A and B shown on drawing #154.

    Door E or. opening similar to C,drawing #10.

    Door jamb,lift #3,mezzanine,is cast iron.

SECOND FLOOR:

    Door D-2, on drawing #150.

    Doors F and F-2 on drawing #150.

    Doors C',similar to C,drawing #150.

    Window J,drawing #150.

    Ceiling lights,on drawing #161.

THIRD STORY:

    Circular transom,window O,and square transom
window P,on drawing #150.

    Doors V,V',W and X,similar to doors C on drawing
No.150.

    Windows L, on drawing #151.

    Windows L',O' and M,similar to L; see scale drawing
No.117.

    The question regarding the approval of the samples
of California white oak for window frames will form
the subject of a separate communication.

              Respectfully,

                        Architect.

3.

DENVER, NEW MINT.

MOD

ENCLOSURE 3705.
FORWARDING.

TREASURY DEPARTMENT,

OFFICE OF THE SUPERVISING ARCHITECT.

Washington, April 28, 1903.

The Superintendent of Construction,

 U. S. Mint (new),

Denver, Col.

Sir:

For your information find herewith copy of office letter of this date, addressed to Messrs. S. Faith and Company, contractors for the mechanical equipment of the building for which you are the Superintendent, advising them of approval of sample of electro-galvanized conduit.

The approved sample will be forwarded to you to-day under separate cover.

Respectfully,

Supervising Architect.

April 2r, 19‑.

Messrs. S. F‑th ‑g Company,

‑427 ‑o ‑ ‑vania Ave.,

P

P‑il‑de'‑ia, ‑‑

Sirs:

‑‑ ‑‑ ‑ ‑‑ ‑tor ‑ ‑ ‑ ‑ ‑ ‑‑ ‑ ‑nt, forwarding
‑ ‑ ‑ ‑‑‑‑p‑v‑‑‑ ‑ ‑ ‑‑ ‑ ‑‑ ‑‑ ‑‑ ‑ ‑
‑‑ ‑‑ ‑ctin ‑‑ ‑‑. ‑ ‑ ‑ ‑ ‑‑‑ ‑‑‑ ‑‑ ‑ ‑ ‑‑ ‑‑
much ‑‑ ‑ ‑ ‑‑p‑‑ ‑ ‑‑ ‑ ‑ ‑‑ ‑‑ , ‑ , ‑‑‑. ‑‑
‑ ‑ ‑ ‑ ‑‑ ‑ ‑‑ ‑ ‑‑ ‑‑ , ‑ ‑‑ ‑‑‑
‑‑ ‑ ‑ ‑, ‑ ‑‑ ‑ ‑‑ ‑ ‑ ‑ ‑ ‑ ‑‑‑ ‑ ‑
‑‑‑ ‑‑ ‑

‑ ‑ ‑‑ ‑‑ ‑.,

(Signed)   ‑. ‑. ‑‑.‑‑.‑‑,

‑JX   ‑uperv‑sing A‑chit‑ect.

TREASURY DEPARTMENT.

OFFICE OF THE SUPERVISING ARCHITECT.

Washington,   April 28, 1903.

The Superintendent of Construction,

      U. S. Mint (New),

         Denver, Col.

Sir:

    Replying to your letter of the 24th instant, with reference
to construction of flue from deposit melting room in basement of
the building for which you are Superintendent, you are advised
that the two vent registers at ceiling in the room referred to,
shown on drawing M-01, and referred to by you, are included in
the contract for mechanical equipment. (See specification, last
part of paragraph 722.)

        Respectfully,

                Supervising Architect.

DENVER MINT (NEW)

RECEIVED NO. 4883.

TREASURY DEPARTMENT,

OFFICE OF THE SUPERVISING ARCHITECT.

Washington,   May 1, 1903.

Superintendent of Construction,
    U.S.Mint Building,(New),
        Denver, Colorado.

Sir:

I enclose herewith, for your information and the files of
your office , copy of a letter this day addressed to Mr. James
A. McGonigle, contractor for the construction of the building
in your charge, relative to sample of California white pine,
which letter explains itself.

Respectfully,

Supervising Architect.

EOP

Mr. James A. McGonigle,
  Leavenworth, Kansas.

Sir:

I have to acknowledge the receipt of your letter of the 27th instant, and, under separate cover, sample of California white pine submitted for approval in connection with your contract for the construction of the New United States Mint building at Denver, Colorado, and you are advised that the white pine, as represented by the sample, is rejected, the grain appearing to be exceedingly coarse and the wood not homogeneous.

In this connection you are advised that since October 25, 1902, you have been in default, under the terms of your contract, in the submission of samples and you are requested to advise this office at once of any reasons which would operate to relieve you from the penalty prescribed for such default, as, unless you thoroughly satisfy this office in regard thereto, the Superintendent will, on the 30th of May, be directed to discontinue the issuance of vouchers until you have complied fully with the terms of your contract relative to samples.

Respectfully,

DENVER NEW MINT.

Inclosure 3317.

TREASURY DEPARTMENT,
OFFICE OF THE SUPERVISING ARCHITECT,

Washington, May 1,1903.

Superintendent of Construction,
      New Mint Building,
            Denver,Colorado.

Sir:

I inclose herewith, for your information and the files of
your office, a copy of Department letter of even date,accepting
the proposal of S.Faith & Company to deduct the sum of one hundred dollars ($100.00) from the amount to be paid them under
their contract for the mechanical equipment of the building in
your charge, to substitute asphalted cast iron pipe, in lieu of
uncoated pipe specified.

The Disbursing Agent has been advised of this deduction.

                              Respectfully,

                                        Supervising Architect.

JSS

TREASURY DEPARTMENT,

OFFICE OF THE SUPERVISING ARCHITECT.

Washington,   April 30, 1903.

F.B.V.

The Superintendent of Construction,

U.S. Mint Building,

Denver,Colorado.

Sir:

In reply to your letter of April 22nd,in reference
to the erection of the furring for the plastered arch over the entrance vestibule to corridor in the building for
which you are the Superintendent of Construction,you are
informed that there are forwarded herewith two prints of
drawing No.149,which,it is believed,will explain the
points in question.

Attention is called to the fact that the soffit of
arch is not paneled,but that the vertical faces are; also
that these faces are over line of column at neck,and that
this drawing supersedes drawing No.112 in this respect.

Respectfully,

Supervising Architect.

B.

TREASURY DEPARTMENT,

OFFICE OF THE SUPERVISING ARCHITECT.

Washington,   May 1, 1903.

Superintendent of Construction,

    U.S.Mint (New),

        Denver, Colorado.

Sir:

    Your communication of the 24th ultimo is acknowledged, transmitting a communication addressed to the office under date of the 23rd ultimo, by Messrs.S.Faith and Company, contractors for the mechanical equipment, in relation to their claim for delays on account of the unfinished condition of work under the contract for the interior finish, &c.,at the building under your charge.

    The statements made in your letter and the enclosure are noted and you are requested to advise Messrs.S.Faith and Company, that all delays of the nature indicated will receive consideration at time of final settlement, under the provisions of the contract bearing thereon.

    It is also desired that you keep record of the delays, in order that you may be able to make demand upon the contractors at such times as may be necessary, to prosecute the work.

    Referring to the backward condition of the work under the contract for the interior finish, you are requested to advise the office, in a special communication, more specifi-

cally in regard thereto, and if it is your judgment that some
decided measures should be taken by the Department to pro-
duce better results, a recommendation should be made by you
covering this feature.

                    Respectfully,

                              Supervising Architect.

DENVER NEW MINT.

TREASURY DEPARTMENT,

OFFICE OF THE SUPERVISING ARCHITECT.

Washington, May 2, 1903.

Superintendent of Construction,
    New Mint,
        Denver, Colorado.

Sir:

You are directed to obtain from Messrs. S.Faith & Company ,
contractors for the mechanical equipment at the building in
your charge, a proposal for supplying five tablets for the
five fan motors constructed and supported similar to tablets
required for pumps,etc., under paragraph #592 of the specification governing their contract; the controlling rheostats,
called for by paragraph #707 of the specification, are to be
mounted on the new tablets, and new breakers and switches are
to be furnished similar to those called for by paragraph #592
mounted on the new boards above-referred to. Upon receipt of
the proposal you are directed to forward it to this Office
with your definite recommendation, upon receipt of which
prompt action will be taken.

                    Respectfully,

                            Supervising Architect.

MTR

F.B.W. 95

TREASURY DEPARTMENT,
OFFICE OF THE SUPERVISING ARCHITECT.

Washington, May 6, 1903.

The Superintendent of Construction,

 U. S. Mint (new),

Denver, Col.

Sir:

For your information find herewith copy of office letter of this day, addressed to S. Faith and Company, contractors for the mechanical equipment of the building for which you are the Superintendent, advising them relative to approval of certain plumbing samples, which will be forwarded to you to-day by express, charges prepaid.

Respectfully,

(Supervising Architect.)

Dec 6, 19 .

Messrs. . Company,
        Pennsylvania Ave e,
          Philadelphia, Pa.

Sirs:

Reply to your letter of the 4th instant, saveing the
f of certa p ples for consideration
 contract for d equipment of
Mint (), Denver, l, t to ffec
lott f 4, tive to ples mentioned in your letter exce lop lak tra standard, and you are advised
o roval of anit phering tra standards for
i inks, as per sample, brass floor flanges, -
p ge submitted rd, -
t oly.

o or nnection the basement be td
and ded for screw connections to waste piping.

Aroved samples of t d floor flange will
be t the uperintend of constrution, with copy of
this letter.

                    Respectfully,

          (Signed)   J.K. TAYLOR
                            Supervising Architect.

DENVER, NEW MINT.

TREASURY DEPARTMENT,

OFFICE OF THE SUPERVISING ARCHITECT

Washington, May 6, 1903.

Superintendent of Construction,
        New Mint,
            Denver, Colorado.

Sir:

I have to acknowledge the receipt of your letter of the
30th ultimo and, under separate cover, of the sample of Colorado Portland cement, referred to therein, taken from material delivered on the site of the building in your charge,
and you are advised that as the sample contains only one quart,
it is difficult to make satisfactory tests with this amount,
and you are directed to forward another sample, containing at
least two (2) quarts, as soon as possible.

Respectfully,

Supervising Architect.

DE:.VER. P.O.

B

Inclosure No.9417.

Mr. Lee Ullery,

    Superintendent of Construction,

        U. S. Mint (new),

           Denver, Colorado.

Sir:

       There is inclosed herewith copy of letter this day
addressed to the Custodian of the Post Office and Court House,
Denver, Colorado, submitting a scheme by which additional space
may be secured for the post-office in that building, etc., and
you are requested to call upon the Custodian and afford him
such assistance as he may desire.

           Respectfully,

                 Supervising Architect.

TREASURY DEPARTMENT,

OFFICE OF THE SUPERVISING ARCHITEC'

Washington, May 6, 1903.

Custodian,

    Post Office and Court House,

        Denver, Colorado.

Sir:

    This office is prepared to give consideration to certain changes in assignments, subject to Departmental approval, at the building in your custody, and repairs incident thereto.

    The scheme is now outlined, with request that you submit your recommendation, and Mr. Ullery has been furnished with a copy of this communication and requested to assist you in the matter and also in obtaining proposals, which you are requested to present; with the understanding, however, that no liability shall be incurred as a charge against the appropriation for the current fiscal year.

    It is the purpose to assign room 2-3, first floor, to wholesale and retail stamp cashier, financial clerk and book-keeper, and to assign room 4 as an auxiliary to the money-order

    On second floor, to remove toilet from room 23 and to cut communicating door between 23 and room adjoining, and to run a partition dividing room 21-22, assigning portion of that room and the former toilet room to the Postmaster, and that portion of the room divided additional to the Clerk of the Court.

    To remove stairway next alley and installing a partition along corridor line and assigning this space to the U.S.Marshal.

On the floor above, to floor over the space where stair has been removed and the room so secured to be subject to later assignments.

In this connection attention is called to authority under date of April 20th to accept the proposal of J. J. Bitter for placing mezzanine floor in money-order department, and in the event that the suggested scheme meets with approval, it may be unnecessary to undertake this work, and you are, therefore, requested to submit your recommendation and to state whether the Department has been as yet committed in any way.

Respectfully,

Supervising Architect.

DENVER, NEW MINT.

MSD

FILE COPIES 3709.
DENVER, COL. G.

TREASURY DEPARTMENT,

OFFICE OF THE SUPERVISING ARCHITECT.

Washington, May 4, 190?.

The Superintendent of Construction,

      U. S. Mint (new),

Denver, Col.

Sir:

For your information find herewith copy of office letter of
this date, addressed to Messrs. S. Faith and Company, contractors
for mechanical equipment of the building for which you are the
Superintendent of Construction, advising them relative to approval
or rejection of plumbing fixtures and appliances which they desire
to use in the work.

The approved samples will be forwarded to you to-day, by express, charges prepaid.

Respectfully,

Supervising Architect.

May 4, 1903.

Messrs. S. Faith and Sons,

    2427 Pennsylvania Ave.,

            Philadelphia, Pa.

Sir:

        Referring to your estimate or mechanical equipment of the
U. S. Post Office, Court House, etc., San Francisco, Cal., you
are advised of the approval of the following-named plumbing fixtures and appliances, as per sample submitted:

        Water Closet Bowl, ⅛ inch outlet: Wolff Manufacturing
            Company's "Superior Syphon Jet";

        Water Closet Bowl, with all outlet: Wolff Manufacturing
            Company's "Superior Syphon Jet";

        Water Closet Seat: Wolff Manufacturing Company's special
            reinforced sort ed oak seat;

        Water Closet Floor Flange, for basement connections only:
            Wolff Manufacturing Company;

        Gasket for water closet connections: Wolff Manufacturing
            Company;

        Urinal Bowl: Wolff Manufacturing Company, "Syphon Jet";

        Urinal Waste Connection Fittings: Wolff Manufacturing Co.;

        Slop Sink: Wolff Manufacturing Company, Class "A", heavy
            porcelain glazed, inside and outside, and fitted with
            brass nickel-plated flushing rim

        Strainer for slop sink: Wolff Manufacturing Company;

        Combination Faucet and connections for slop sink (except
            that look shield onto valves must be provided in sup-
            ply connections): Wolff Manufacturing Company;

        Lavatory Bowl: Wolff Manufacturing Company;

Lavatory Brackets Wolff Manufacturing Company;

Bon-Syphon Lavatory Trap (except that trap furnished
must be 1-1/2" for the single and two-basin lavateries
and 2" for the five-basin lavatory, as required by the
specification); "Ideal", Ideal Manufacturing Company;

Double Coat Hook: Wolff Manufacturing Company;

Buffer for Water Closet Door: Wolff Manufacturing Company;

Flushing Valve for Water Closet: Wolff Manufacturing Co.;

Flushing Valve for Urinal: Wolff Manufacturing Company;

Flushing Valve for Slop Sink: Wolff Manufacturing Company;
All of this, approved submitted, however, are subject
to the guarantee required by paragraphs 104, 105, and
106 of the specification, and be provided with finished brass, the vitly nickel-plated handles, convenient-
ly fastened to the operating levers as required by
paragraph 99 of specification, and finished steel,
nickel-plated ground joint union must also be provided
on the supply connection to each flushing valve between the flushing valve and cut-off valve, as required
by paragraph 103 of specification.

The following used samples submitted by you are rejected
for the reasons hereinafter stated, and you are requested to submit satisfactory samples in their place:

Self-Closing Lavatory Faucet: Wolff Manufacturing Company,
"Gielow", with round arms. Same do not operate
satisfactorily. Lavatory faucets must be adjusted to
operate easily, with 60 lbs. water pressure on the system, and the handles of faucet should have wider rims;

Nickel-Plated Brass Tubing, same not being of required thick-
ness for waste piping. not less than 18 B.W. gauge required by specification;

Nickel-Plated Floor and Wall Plates: same are not cast brass
required by paragraphs 147 and 148 of specification;

You are requested to furnish samples of the following-named additional plumbing appliances, etc., as required by paragraph 296 of specifications:

One 4 o.c. floor flange for screw jointed connection;

Non-siphoning trap standard for slop sink;

Toilet Paper holder;

One 1-1/4" finished brass, nickel-plated gate valve with lock shield;

Fire Hose Reel or Rack;

Fire Hose;

One complete standard for water closet partition, including top piece bolt;

One angle retaining bar be water closet partition;

One socket fastening for water closet partition;

One hinge for water closet door;

One bolt and stop for water closet door;

One 14" long section of #16 B. & S. gauge brass, nickel-plated tubing, for water closet enclosure framing;

One 12" section brass, nickel-plated water pipe, "Standard" U. S. pipe gauge;

One 12" long section of 2" diameter galvanized wrought iron or steel lead lined pipe;

One 12" long section of 4" diameter cast iron lead lined pipe.

Approved samples will be sent to the Superintendent of Construction, and rejected samples returned to you, by express, collect

Respectfully,

Supervising Architect.

DENVER, NEW MINT.

TREASURY DEPARTMENT,

OFFICE OF THE SUPERVISING ARCHITECT

Washington,   May 5, 1903,

Superintendent of Construction,

      Mint Building,

         Denver, Colorado.

Sir:-

     I have to advise you that a request has this day been made for a remittance to the Disbursing Agent of the building in your charge, in the sum of...........$40,000.00, under his new bond approved May 1, 1903, from the appropriation for "Mint Building, Denver, Colorado," to enable him to make payment of authorized expenditures.

               Respectfully,

                            Chief Executive Officer.

FD

U. S. COURT HOUSE AND POST OFFICE,

Pueblo,Colo.,May 7,1903.

Mr. Lee Ullery,

    Sup't of Construction,

        U.S.Mint Building, Denver Colo.

Dear Sir:--

    Your communication of 6th inst. at hand; I enclose herewith the
bill of particulars referred to, and have to report that the work of
The Piper Bros. Co. will be completed by the end of this month, but
that they do not expect final inspection until the lawn has been given
time to show whether the work has been successful as to the re-sod-
ding. Probably the first week in June is as early as it would be possible to judge of the quality of the lawn improvements.

        Respectfully,

        Ed Osgood

        Acting Custodian

RECEIVED at 1114 to 1116 17th St., Denver, Colo.   NEVER CLOSED.

540 CH RT N 27 Pd Govt.

Chicago, May 13

Mr. Lee Ullery,

　　　　　Supt of Construction U Mint Bldg. Denver, Col.

Leach case postponed Do not come until further notice.

　　　　　F H Rethea,

　　　　　　　　United States Attorney

　　　710p.

DENVER, NEW MINT.

TREASURY DEPARTMENT,

OFFICE OF THE SUPERVISING ARCHITECT

Washington, May 11, 1903.

Superintendent of Construction,
    New Mint,
        Denver, Colorado.

Sir:

    You are directed to obtain from the electrical contractors
at the building in your charge a proposal for the supply and
installation of a 1 1/4" conduit with #4 B. & S. gauge con-
ductor running from junction box A-8 on power circuit #18,
drawing E.W.89, in floor construction, a distance of about
14'0" north, then down on east face of wall between heater
and engine rooms to a point about 5'6" above heater room
floor, and forward it to this Office with your definite recommendation.

                    Respectfully,

                                Supervising Architect.

DENVER NEW MINT.

TREASURY DEPARTMENT,

OFFICE OF THE SUPERVISING ARCHITECT.

Washington, May 14, 1903.

Superintendent of Construction,
   New Mint Building,
      Denver, Colorado.

Sir:

I inclose herewith, for your information and the files
of your office, a copy of Department letter of even date, accepting the proposal of Messrs. S.Faith & Company, the contractors for the mechanical equipment of the building in your
charge, to make certain substitution of air compressors,etc.,
without additional cost to the Government, all as stated in
detail in said letter of acceptance, and there is forwarded
you, under separate cover, a copy of drawings Nos. H-203 and
H-204, for the files of your office and your guidance in accepting the work.

                            Respectfully,

                                    Supervising Architect.

MTR

                                              ― 14, 1903.

Messrs. ?. ?aith & Company,
        ??? ?uilding,
          Denver, Colorado.

Gentlemen:

        In view of the public exigency which requires the
immediate performance of the work, your proposal dated ??? 11,
190?, is hereby accepted, to substitute, without additional
cost to the Government, under ?our contract, dated A???? ?,
1902, for t?? mechanical equipment of the New Mint Building in ??
Denver, Colorado, two ?l? ten ??i-, two-stage air comp????ors,
with silent chain drive, in lieu of the Stillwell-Pierce &
Smith-Ville Company's compressors, approved by Department letter of August 9, 1902, the change being made as it i? ???er-
stood the _prompt_ delivery of the appliance original, approved can
not b? ?.de, all as set forth in your proposal ??. the specification attached thereto, and the two drawings submitted
to and approved; that of the Clayton air compressor being
been given Office number ?/20? ??? ??t showing location of
air compressor and compressed air tanks and house pumps and
air pressure tank, etc., number R-204. On? copy of each of the
drawings is forwarded you herewith and one will be sent to
the Superintendent of Construction for the files of his office
and his guidance in accepting the work.

        It is understood and agreed that this acceptance is
??t to affect the time for the completion of the entire work
as fixed in the original contract; that the same is without

prejudice to any and all rights of the United States thereunder;
and without prejudice, also, to the rights of the United States
against the sureties on the bond executed for the faithful
fulfillment of the contract.

Please promptly acknowledge the receipt of this letter,
a copy of which will be forwarded to the Superintendent of
Construction, for his information.

Respectfully,

Assistant Secretary.

A
JCP

MTR

Letter head of S. Faith & Company.

Philadelphia, May 11, 1903.

Specifications covering the two 9 x 5½ x 9 Clayton duplex motor driven air compressors for the Denver Mint, Denver, Colo.

The compressors are to be of the Duplex type having

9" Low pressure air cylinder

5½" high pressure air cylinder, all of 9" stroke, mounted on a bedplate extended to receive motor. All castings to be made of close grained gray iron and well finished. The connection between motor drive to be made of special gears. The detail construction is as follows:

The 9" piston has four cast iron backing rings sprung in. The 5½" piston consists of body, bull ring and follower and four cast iron backing rings, which are turned 5½" and pressed against the cylinder wall of two cast iron spring rings. The low pressure discharge and suction valves are hard rubber faced and are of the flat disc. type. The valve seats are of bronze and screwed into the desk on a fine taper thread, making the maximum amount of clearance at the end of the cylinder. The height pressure discharge and suction valves are conical and made of bronze, well guided in their seats. The high pressure air cylinder is water jacketed.

The diameter of the main shaft is 2½", length of bearings 5" x 2½", crosshead pins being two pins of 1¼" diameter by 2¼".

7'

TREASURY DEPARTMENT,

OFFICE OF THE SUPERVISING ARCHITECT.

Washington, May 13, 1903.

614

E.A.C.

The Superintendent of Construction,

U. S. Mint (New),

Denver, Col.

Sir:

For your information find herewith copy of office letter of
this date, addressed to Messrs. S. Faith and Company, contractors
for the mechanical equipment of the building for which you are
the Superintendent of Construction, relative to soapstone sinks
to be supplied under said contract.

Respectfully,

Supervising Architect.

May 24, 190-.

Messrs. R. Faith and Company,
      _ _7 Pennsylvania Avenue,

      Y   Philadelphia, Pa.

Sirs:

        Replying to your letter of the 11th instant, relative to
_ _ _ _ _ _ sinks to be supplied under your contract for mechanical _ _ _ _ _ _ _ _ _ _. Mint (new), Denver, Colo., you are
_ _ _ _ _ _ _ _ _ _ o. 100 has no detail drawings or cuts of the
s _ _ _ _ _ _ _ _ required, but the description of said sinks in
_ _ _ _ _ _ _ _ _ _ to _ _ of the specification governing the work
_ _ _ _ _ _ _ _ _ _ _ _ _ _ _ order to enable us to build same in
_ _ _ _ _ _ _ _ _ _ _ _.

        _ _ _ _ _ _ _ the description referred to, you are ad-
vised _ _ t the bottom of each of the soapstone sinks should be
_ _ _ _ _ _ _ slated, _ _ s to drain towards the waste outlet.

                Respectfully,

        (Signed)   J. K. TAYLOR
                           Supervising Architect.

TREASURY DEPARTMENT,

OFFICE OF THE SUPERVISING ARCHITECT.

Washington, May 13, 1903.

Superintendent of Construction,
New Mint,
Denver, Colorado.

Sir:

You are directed to obtain from the contractor for the mechanical equipment for the building in your charge, a proposal for the supply and installation of two 8" vibrating electric gongs with three push buttons, wire tubing, etc., and a battery of four Leclanche type cells for the bell at front entrance, and eight cells for bell at back entrance, or a sufficient number of cells for the satisfactory operation of each bell. Gongs to be highly polished, other parts neatly finished in black enamel, and the bells to be of different pitch. The push buttons to be of ornamental design and finished in bronze; the button at front entrance to be placed on west side of doorway on outer granite reveal. For the gong at back door there must be two buttons, one at the door on east side, and one at east entrance of alley, on north side of gateway, and placed about 5'0" above grade. The bell for front entrance to be placed about 10'0" above floor in northwest corner of entrance hall and back of column; the bell for rear entrance to be placed on east side of doorway and about 8'0" above floor. Battery for bell at front entrance to be placed on a shelf in closet of Cashier's room; and for the bell at back entrance, to be placed in a neat wood case on south wall of corridor and near bell. Wires in the building to be run

in tubing and from button at alley gate in steel conduit properly protected from corrosion.   Upon receipt of said proposal,
you are directed to forward it to this Office with your definite recommendation.

Respectfully,

Supervising Architect.

TREASURY DEPARTMENT,

OFFICE OF THE SUPERVISING ARCHITECT.

Washington, May 14, 1903.

Z.A.C. 66

The Superintendent of Construction,

U. S. Mint (new),

Denver, Col.

Sir:

For your information in herewith copy of office letter of this date, addressed to Messrs. S. Faith and Company, contractors for the mechanical equipment of the building for which you are the Superintendent of Construction, advising them relative to approval or rejection of certain electrical appliances and materials which they desire to use in the work.

The approved samples (4) will be forwarded to you to-day, by express, charges prepaid.

Respectfully,

Supervising Architect.

Messrs. .. Faith and Company,

        .... / Penn-ylvania Ave.,

    .   P ..adelphia, .e.

'irs:

      Receipt is acknowledged of your letter of the .th instant,
. ..r.... ... consideration certain samples incident to ... ..c-
....r .. ... contract for mechanical equipment of ...
.... .howi, Denver, Col., and you are advised that the
.... - ...g ... . re approved:

               Ceiling outlet ....;
               Wire;

      ... . samples .re rejected, for ... reasons
...vo..

               Poor work: .. inferior workmanship;
               ..... red ... ..; .... and inharp....

      ... rejected ..mpl...   ...   .ss,
..-..... collect, .nd you   ...   .
.... samples f.... ir .o.r.. co..... . .if......... ... .

      ... approved samples .... to the Superintendent at
... .ail....., with copy of this letter.

                         Respectfully,

               (Signed)   .. .. TAYLOR
                                     Supervising Architect.

Philadelphia., May 16th,1903.

Superintendent of Construction,

New Mint, Denver, Colo.

Sir:-

We propose to furnish in connection with our contract for
the Mechanical Equipment for the U.S.Mint (New), Denver, Colorado, five
tablets for the five fan motors constructed and supported similar to
tablets required for pumps,etc., under paragraph #592 of the specification governing the above contract. The controlling rheostats,called
for by paragraph #707 of the specifications,are to be mounted on the
new tablets, and new breakers and switches are to be furnished similar
to those called for by paragraph 592 mounted on the new boards above
referred to,for the sum of Five hundred and fifty Dollars ($550.). The
instruments called for are of a high grade and require special work.

Respectfully,

(Signed) S.Frith & Co.

Mr. Lee Ullery,

    Superintendent of Construction,Mint Building,

        Denver, Colo.

Sir:-

    I hereby propose to remove the louvres and put in place the shutters, mechanism &c. and additional gutters of skylight of the Mint Building in this city in accordance with drawing No. 139 and and your letter of Nov. 25th, 1902 for the sum of one thousand three hundred eighty five ($1385.00) Dollars.

                                 Contractor.

Mr. Lee Ullery,

    Supt. of Construction, Mint Building,

        Denver, Colo.

Sir:-

    I hereby propose to excavate for and put in place the extra
depth of concrete foundations under chimneys and columns in the
Mint Building in this city as requested by your letter of the 12th
instant for Fifty ($50.00) Dollars.

                                    James A. McCough

                              Contractor.

Mr. Lee Ullery,

    Supt. of Construction, Mint Building,

        Denver, Colo.

Sir:-

    I hereby propose to put in place the double terra cotta partition in basement between columns Nos. 4 and 5 of the Mint Building in this city as requested in your letter of the 17th ultimofo thirty three ($33.00) Dollars.

                                    James A. Wilburn

                            Contractor.

Mr. Lee Ullery,

    Supt. of Construction, Mint Building,

         Denver, Colo.

Sir:-

    I hereby propose to furnish and put in place the three registers in furred ceilings of the Furnice and Acid Laboratory rooms of the Mint Building in this city as requested in your letter of the 2nd ultimo, for the sum of Sixty nine ($69.00) Dollars.

James A. McGuigl

        Contractor.

Mr. Lee Ullery,

    Supt. of Construction, Mint Building,

          Denver, Colo.

Sir:-

    I hereby propose to put in place the plank walks, platforms
&c. and prepare the openings in the terra cotta partitions above
furred ceilings of first and second stories of the Mint Building,
in this city in accordance with your letter of the 13th, instant
and blue prints Nos. 1 and 2? for the sum of Three hundred($300.00)
Dollars.

                                                Contractor.

DENVER NEW MINT.

Incloe re 4827.

TREASURY DEPARTMENT

WASHINGTON   May 20, 1903.

Superintendent of Construction,
    New Mint Building,
        Denver, Colorado.

Sir:

I inclose herewith, for your information and the files
of your office, a copy of a letter of even date, which explains
itself, addressed to the contractor for the completion of the
building in your charge, relative to his default in the matter of
submission of samples required, and you are directed to suspend
the issuance of vouchers to him for payments on account of the
work, until receipt of further instructions from this Office.

Respectfully,

Supervising Architect.

JSS

DENVER NEW MINT.

Nov 20,1908.

Mr. James A. Sommerville,
        Ex C Superintendentof Construction,New Mint Building,
            Denver,Colorado.

SIR:

        Referring to my late letter to you of the 1st instant,relative
to your default in the matter of samples required in connection
with your contract for the completion of the new Mint Building at
Denver,Colorado, and your letter of the 14th instant, you are
advised that the Superintendent of Construction has been directed
to suspend the issuance of vouchers to you for payments on account of the work during such time as the default continues.

                Respectfully,

                        Supervising Architect.

DENVER, NEW MINT.

Inclosure 4836.

TREASURY DEPARTMENT

WASHINGTON May 22, 1903.

Superintendent of Construction,
   New Mint Building,
      Denver, Colorado.

Sir:

I inclose herewith, for your information and the files of your office, a copy of a letter of even date, addressed to the contractors for the vaults for the building in your charge, relative to the decoration on the vault doors, which letter explains itself.

Respectfully,

(Supervising Architect.

JSS

May ,19 .

          ...   Company,
    .... , ...

          ... ... to your contract for the vaults for the
     .. ..,........, and to the re........ of the ....
....al .... p...... o ... vault doors,...
.. ..
.. .., it .. .., ..
... ... , ...
... ... , ... , ...
... .. , ... oxidized silver ... .
.. .., ... to ... .
. .. United States .. ..Treasury ...., ...
... .ion. The silver ...... be not ...
... 1/32" ...., backed up by suitable ...... and with concealed
fastening. Upon receipt of your .. ..
.... consideration.

                         Respectfully,

                                         Supervising Architec .

   JSS

TREASURY DEPARTMENT

WASHINGTON **May 22, 1903.**

Superintendent of Construction,
New Mint Building,
Denver, Colorado.

Sir:

I have to advise you that your suggestion as to the floors
of the two refinery rooms in the second story of the building
in your charge, contained in your letter of the 15th instant, is
approved; and you are, therefore, requested to obtain from Mr. James
A. McGonigle, the contractor for the completion of the building,
a proposal to substitute hard Alberene stone, in lieu of the
granite specified, for the floors of these two rooms, and, also, for
the base in the laboratories, and forward the same to this Office
with your definite recommendation.

Respectfully,

Supervising Architect.

DENVER NEW MINT.

TREASURY DEPARTMENT

WASHINGTON ,May 25, 1903.

Superintendent of Construction,
     New Mint,
          Denver, Colorado.

Sir:

   I have to acknowledge the receipt of your letter of the
19th instant and you are directed to obtain from the contractors
a proposal for terra cotta fireproofing over vault B-C in
the building in your charge, and forward it to this Office
with your definite recommendation.

               Respectfully,

                              Supervising Architect.

MTR

DENVER MINT (NEW)

(FORWARDING)

TREASURY DEPARTMENT

F.B.V.

WASHINGTON May 27, 1903.

The Superintendent of Construction,

United States Mint Building,

Denver,Colorado.

Sir:

The Office is in receipt of your letter of the 18th instant,and,in accordance with the request therein contained,there has this day been forwarded you,under separate cover,one print of drawing No.140 for the building of which you are the Superintendent of Construction.

Respectfully,

Supervising Architect.

B.

DENVER NEW MINT.

Inclosure 4948.

TREASURY DEPARTMENT

WASHINGTON May 28, 1903.

Superintendent of Construction,
   New Mint Building,
     Denver, Colorado.

Sir:

I inclose herewith, for your information and the files of your office, a copy of Department letter of even date, accepting the proposal of James A. McGonigle, as an addition to his contract for the completion of the building in your charge, in amount thirty-three dollars ($33.00), to place a double 4" terra cotta partition in the basement, between columns 4 and 5, as stated in the said acceptance.

You are hereby authorized to certify and issue vouchers on account of the work, as required by the terms of the contract and the printed "Instructions to Superintendents", payment of which vouchers the Disbursing Agent has been authorized to make from the appropriation for Mint Building, Denver, Colorado.

                   Respectfully,

                          Acting Supervising Architect.

JBB

May 20, 1903.

P. Mr. A. _____ fris,
_____ ___, ___ ___.

Sir:

In view of the statement and recommendation contained in letter of the 2nd instant, from the Superintendent of Construction of the new mint building at Denver, Colorado, your approval, of the same date, written at Denver, Colorado, in ___ thirty-three dollars ($33.00), is hereby accepted _____ a ___ in 4" terra cotta partition in basement, _____ columns 4 and 5, as described in the Superintendent's letter to you of the 17th instant, a _____ _____ requiring _____ ____, _____ is to be an _____ _____ to _____ contract, dated August __, 1902, for the completion of the building.

It is _____ _____ that this acceptance is not to affect the time for the completion of the work, as required by the terms of your contract; but the same is without prejudice to _____ and all rights of the United States thereunder; and _____ prejudice, also, to any and all rights of the United States against the sureties on the bond executed for the faithful fulfillment of the contract.

Please acknowledge the receipt of this letter.

Respectfully,

— Acting Secretary.

T.
J.T.P.
JSC

INCLOSURE 4693. **TREASURY DEPARTMENT**

WASHINGTON May 28, 1903.

Superintendent of Construction,
    New Mint,
        Denver, Colorado.

Sir:

    I inclose herewith, for your information and the files
of your office, a copy of a letter this day addressed to the
contractor for the construction of the building in your charge,
and the samples of oak and pine, mentioned therein as being
approved, are forwarded you, under separate cover, being for
the files of your office and your guidance in accepting the
work.

                Respectfully,

                    Acting Supervising Architect .

Mr. Thomas A. McGonigle,
    Leavenworth, Kansas.

Sir:

    Referring to your letter of the 14th instant, submitting
samples for approval in connection with your contract for the
completion of the New Mint building at Denver, Colorado, you
are advised that the following, as represented by the samples,
are approved as to quality of wood and color of finish, it
being understood that all finish is to be applied in strict
accordance with the requirements of the specification, and the
samples forwarded to the superintendent of Construction for
the files of his office and his guidance in accepting the
work, via:

        White oak.
        Hard pine.

                        Respectfully,

                                Acting Supervising Architect.

TREASURY DEPARTMENT

WASHINGTON May 28, 1905.

ENCLOSURE 2490.
FORWARDING.

The Superintendent of Construction,

U. S. Mint (new),

Denver, Col.

Sir:

For your information find herewith copy of office letter
of this date, addressed to Messrs. S. Faith and Company, contractors for mechanical equipment of the building for which
you are the Superintendent of Construction, approving certain
plumbing samples (waste piping, and floor and wall plates),
which will be forwarded to you to-day, by mail, under separate
cover.

Respectfully,

Acting Supervising Architect.

Messrs. S. Faith and Company,

nnn Par leard., ly. la,

?   Philadelphia, Pa.

Sir:

Referring to your contract for specialized equipment of the
n. n. was (ex), however, ... contract is expressed as of con-
.... after ... ... institutes, we pr im de-
vised a fi ...:

... ... from x from fittings or the
faucet, which are three nickel-plated four and sell finish, do
so as the predictod.

This article is ... is rejected, so the ...
temporary use. The principle of the range is satisfactory,
but the construction is defective at the following-named points:

1.   The handle is defective in finish, and not properly
fitted and secured to the stem;

2.   The cap just below the handle is too light a pattern,
as there is not thread enough on the body of faucet to
secure the cap properly in place when the spindle is
turned to the left;

3.   The joint in body of faucet should be a ground union
joint, so that faucet can be taken apart readily for repairs.

Sample of 1-1/4" diameter brass tubing is also rejected, as
no tubing of that gauge is required.

The approved samples (waste Pping and floor and wall plates)
will ... ... the Superintendent of Construction at the building.
... ... referred to (faucet and 1-1/4" tubing) will be ... ... by express, charges collect;
... ... requested to ... ... as possible a satisfactory
... ... that, ... additional plumbing
... ... of-
... ...

(Signed)   .K.TAYLOR

TREASURY DEPARTMENT

WASHINGTON May 28, 1903 .

Superintendent of Construction,
New Mint,
Denver, Colorado.

Sir:

I have to acknowledge the receipt of your letter of the 21st instant, in which you suggest that it is not necessary to place asphalt,required by the contract of Mr.James A.Mc Gonigle for the completion of the building in your charge,for retaining wall on south of lot, which you state will be built of concrete, and you are advised that after careful considera- tion it is deemed best to require the contractor to perform the work as required by the specification.

Respectfully,

Acting Supervising Architect.

Supervising Architect.

Supervising Architect

Name of Inspector Thompson. not to be placed on pay roll

Correspondence regarding. marble cornice in corridor

Regarding rejection of sample of terrazzo

" openings for flues near column No 8

Acceptance of proposal for repairing roof gutters & down pipes

Shop drawings for ornamental iron

Regarding width of coping walls on No. 13th Street

Albcrene Stone Company of N.Y. can supply stone named

Correspondence regarding marble cornice in corridor

Approving sample of raw linseed oil

Information regarding certain interior finish work

Approving sample of electro-galvanized conduit

Two men registers in Defect Melting Room in M.E. central

Rejecting California White Pine

Accepting proposal to substitute asphalted cast iron pipe

Related to plastering arch over entrance vestibule

" claim for delays by St Faith & Co

Requesting proposal for fire tablets for fan motors

Approving certain plumbing samples

Requesting two quarts of 68/0 Portland cement

Regarding arrangement for additional space at Post Office

" approval, &c. plumbing samples

Requesting proposal for 1¼" conduit with #4 B&S gauge

Supervising Architect

(Bethea J H

S Faith & Company

Proposal for repairing down spouts
  "   of   "   " + roof gutter
    to substitute asphalted cast iron pipe.
Recording delays in work
Proposal for five stable for four motors, &c/

James A. McGonigle

Proposal for steel furring, &c, in attic

" " magnabests blocks in Coming Room

Discrepancies in details for marble work

Relative to batter of wall on south side

Proposal for shutters, mechanism, gutters, &c. of skylight

" " extra depth of foundation under chimneys

" " double 4" T.C. partition in basement

" " three registers in ceiling of Acid Laboratory

" " plank walk over furred ceilings

s
r